KNOWING YOUR CIVIL RIGHTS

A TRUE BOOK®

by
Christin Ditchfield

Children's Press®
A Division of Scholastic Inc.

New York Toronto London Auckland Sydne~~~~
Mexico City New Delhi Hong Kong ~~~~~~~~
Danbury, Connecticut

Signing a petition is a way of exercising one's civil rights.

Reading Consultant
Jeanne Clidas, Ph.D.
*National Reading Consultant
and Professor of Reading,
SUNY Brockport*

Content Consultant
Jonathan Riehl, J.D.
*Graduate Instructor,
Communications Studies
University of North Carolina,
Chapel Hill*

Library of Congress Cataloging-in-Publication Data

Ditchfield, Christin.
    Knowing your civil rights / by Christin Ditchfield.
        v. cm. — (A true book)
    Includes bibliographical references.
    Contents: Do you know your civil rights? — The Bill of rights —
The civil rights movement — Equal rights for everyone —
Respecting our civil rights.
    ISBN 0-516-22800-5 (lib. bdg.)   0-516-27910-6 (pbk.)
    1. Civil rights—United States—Juvenile literature. 2. Civil
rights movements—United States—History—20th century—Juvenile
literature. [1. Civil rights. 2. Civil rights movements—History—
20th century.]
I. Title. II. Series.
    KF4750.D49 2004
    342.7308'5—dc22
                                                    2003022704

CHILDREN'S PRESS, and A TRUE BOOK™, and associated logos are
trademarks and or registered trademarks of Scholastic Library Publishing.
SCHOLASTIC and associated logos are trademarks and or registered
trademarks of Scholastic Inc.
1 2 3 4 5 6 7 8 9 10 R 13 12 11 10 09 08 07 06 05 04

Contents

Civil rights are guaranteed to all U.S. citizens.

Do You Know Your Civil Rights?

It makes no difference whether you are male or female, young or old. The way you look does not matter, nor does your family background or your religious beliefs. As a member of your community, you have the right to freedom and equal

treatment under the law. These are your civil rights.

You exercise your civil rights when you speak out about an important issue or vote on laws that will affect you. Your civil rights give you freedom to attend religious services. They protect your privacy and allow you to defend yourself. **Citizens** of the United States have many freedoms and responsibilities.

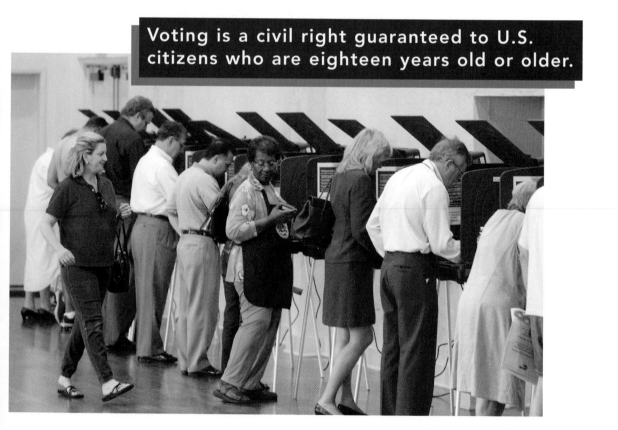

Voting is a civil right guaranteed to U.S. citizens who are eighteen years old or older.

When the United States of America became a country, its leaders created a **document** called the Constitution. The Constitution lays out the rules for the American system of government. The first leaders of the United States believed that individual freedom was one of the most important **principles** of government. They wanted to be sure that the new government they were creating would protect

A painting showing United States leaders writing the U.S. Constitution

the rights and freedoms of its citizens.

At first, the Constitution did not specifically list all of these freedoms. This concerned many people. So new laws,

The Bill of Rights

called amendments, were added. The first ten amendments to the Constitution are known as the Bill of Rights.

The Bill of Rights

The First Amendment to the
U.S. Constitution guarantees
U.S. citizens several liberties,
including freedom of speech.
Freedom of speech is the freedom to express ideas. It means
people may express their opinions in public speeches and
debates. They can share their

Freedom of speech allows people to express their opinions in many different ways.

thoughts in books, magazines, newspapers, movies, music, radio, and television. Freedom of speech even includes "speech acts"—when people show what they think by carrying signs or wearing symbols.

The First Amendment also gives U.S. citizens freedom of the press and the freedom to assemble peacefully. Neighbors can gather together to discuss important issues that affect their community. They can sign **petitions** demanding that unfair laws be changed. Journalists can criticize the government. They can report the news as

A television reporter covering a protest against government policies

they see it, regardless of whether the government approves of what they say.

In addition, the First Amendment grants citizens freedom of religion. In some countries, the government decides what religion its citizens must follow. American citizens may worship any way they please, and they are free to share their religious faith with others.

People in the United States have the right to practice any religion they choose.

The Second Amendment protects the right of citizens to "bear arms," or own guns. The Third and Fourth Amendments protect citizens' privacy. Citizens cannot be forced to house soldiers. The police cannot search a person's home, car, or personal belongings without just cause—without good reason to believe a person is involved in illegal activity. Often, police must get a warrant, a legal document

The Bill of Rights states that the police cannot search a person's property without just cause.

signed by a judge that grants permission for the search.

The Fifth, Sixth, Seventh, and Eighth Amendments all protect the rights of the **accused**. A person cannot be forced to **confess** to a crime.

A person accused of a crime in the United States has the right to receive advice from a lawyer.

Accused citizens have the right to receive advice from a lawyer. They have the right to a fair and speedy trial. The government may not inflict cruel and unusual punishment on criminals. In addition to the protections of these amendments, American law has always said that a person is considered innocent until he or she is proven guilty.

The Ninth Amendment states that citizens have other rights not specifically mentioned in the Constitution. These rights are just as important. The government cannot pass new laws that take away the rights listed in the first eight amendments.

The Civil Rights Movement

The Bill of Rights became law in 1791. The Constitution guaranteed civil rights to all U.S. citizens. In reality, however, many people were denied their civil rights. Slavery was legal in the United States until 1865. After slavery ended, most African-Americans were still

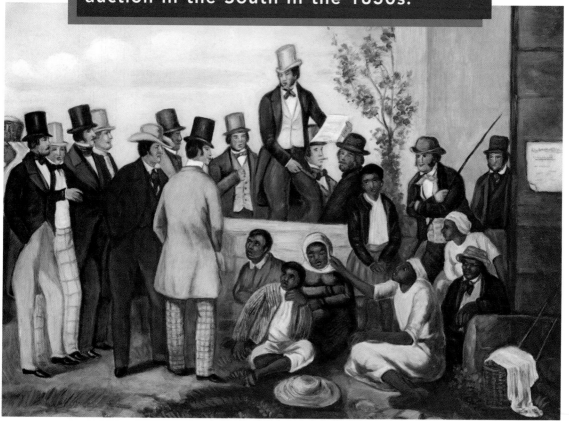

treated differently than whites. Many blacks were not allowed to vote until 1868, when the

Fifteenth Amendment was passed. Even after that, blacks were often prevented from voting.

Almost one hundred years later, blacks were still being treated like second-class citizens. Many communities adopted segregation, the practice of separating blacks and whites. Blacks and whites lived in separate neighbor-hoods. There were schools for black children and schools for

A segregated drinking fountain in the South in the 1950s

white children. Blacks had to sit in the back of city buses. They could not use "white" restrooms or water fountains in public buildings. They were not allowed to enter many stores, restaurants, and hotels. Other businesses forced blacks to use separate entrances or remain in separate parts of buildings, away from white customers. Local laws supported this segregation.

The civil rights movement began in the 1960s. All over the United States, people who opposed segregation began **protesting** in the streets. African-Americans organized

During the civil rights movement of the 1960s, people demonstrated for the rights of African-Americans.

boycotts. They refused to ride in segregated buses. They stopped shopping in stores where they were treated disrespectfully. People marched through towns carrying signs and banners. They demanded that unfair laws be changed.

Finally, in 1964, President Lyndon B. Johnson signed the Civil Rights Act. Segregation was no longer legal. The federal government said once and for all that all citizens had

President Johnson hands his pen to civil-rights leader Martin Luther King Jr. just after signing the Civil Rights Act of 1964.

the same rights and privileges under the law, regardless of the color of their skin.

"I Have a Dream"

On August 28, 1963, civil-rights leader Martin Luther King Jr. addressed a crowd of more than 200,000 protesters in Washington, D.C. In his famous speech, King talked about his dreams for the future of the United States. He hoped the day would come when all Americans would be able to enjoy the rights guaranteed to them by the Constitution. King said, "I have a dream that my four little children will one day live in a nation where they will not be judged by the color of their skin, but by the content of their character."

Equal Rights for Everyone

African-Americans are not the only citizens whose civil rights have been ignored. For many years, women were not allowed to own property. They could not attend certain schools and universities. Women could not vote or run for public office. They could

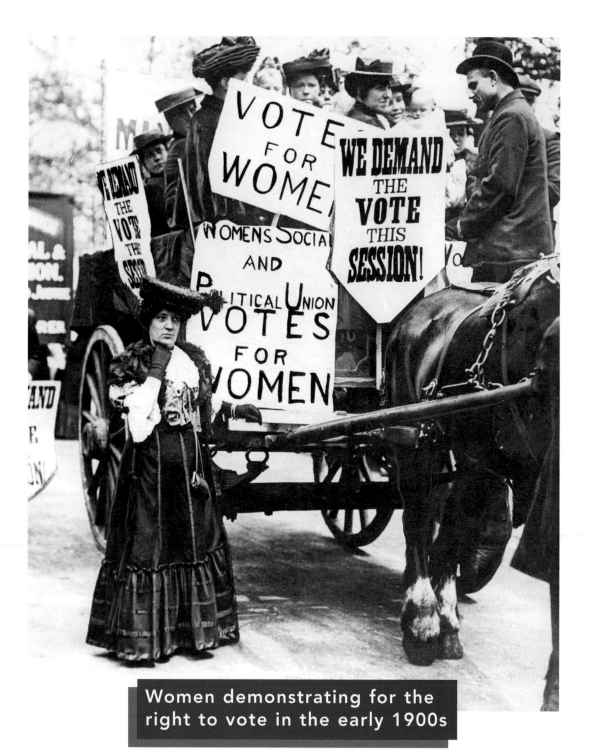

Women demonstrating for the right to vote in the early 1900s

Women have fought hard for the right to enter professions that were once open only to men.

not compete in sporting events, such as the Olympic Games. Women were not permitted to hold certain types of jobs. They did not get paid as much as men did, even when they did the same work.

In 1920, the Nineteenth Amendment gave women the right to vote. Ever since, American women have been working to achieve equality in society: equal opportunity, equal responsibility, equal pay.

In recent years, the U.S. government has passed laws to defend the rights of senior citizens. These laws protect

33

In the United States, a senior citizen cannot be fired from a job simply because of his or her age.

the elderly from being cheated, mistreated, or abused. Older workers cannot be fired from their jobs or forced to retire simply because of their age.

In 1990, the Americans with Disabilities Act was passed. This law requires schools, restaurants, and businesses to be **accessible** to people with disabilities. They must provide

By law, people with disabilities must have access to public transportation. Here, a public bus is equipped with a wheelchair lift.

handicapped parking spaces, wheelchair ramps, and wider entrances and hallways. Employers cannot refuse to hire someone simply because he or she has a disability.

All over the country, students are discovering their civil rights. They exercise free speech by protesting school policies, wearing certain symbols, or writing their opinions in school newspapers. Students who are concerned about their privacy

Kids can exercise their civil rights by writing to government leaders about issues that concern them.

have objected to locker searches and drug testing. Some refuse to say the Pledge of Allegiance because it includes the phrase "under God." Others insist they have a right to pray and share their faith on their school campus.

"You Have the Right

According to the Constitution, people accused of crimes cannot be forced to confess or admit their guilt. Before speaking to police, they have the right to receive advice from an attorney.

In 1963, a man named Ernesto Miranda admitted committing a violent crime. He escaped punishment, however, because the police had not told him that it was his right to refuse to answer their questions.

Ernesto Miranda

Ever since the Miranda case, police officers have been required to read criminal suspects the Miranda Warning, which advises them of their civil rights.

to Remain Silent"

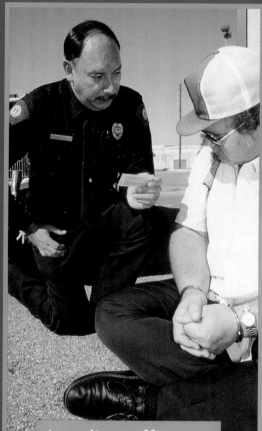

A police officer reading the Miranda Warning during an arrest

When an officer makes an arrest, he or she begins, "You have the right to remain silent . . ."

Miranda Warning

You have the right to remain silent. Anything you say can and will be used against you in a court of law. You have the right to speak to an attorney, and to have an attorney present during any questioning. If you cannot afford a lawyer, one will be provided for you at government expense.

Respecting Our Civil Rights

It is important for all of us to understand our civil rights. We need to know what freedoms we have and how we can use them. We also need to understand our responsibilities. Just because we are free to do something does not mean that

A woman expresses her views at a town meeting as others listen respectfully.

we should do it. We must use our freedom wisely. While we exercise our own civil rights, we should take care to respect the rights of others.

From time to time, those freedoms will be in danger. The United States has come under attack. Foreign countries have tried to limit or control its freedom. The country's own leaders have sometimes suggested new laws to be added to the Constitution—laws that would take away or restrict civil rights. People need to be alert to the danger. United States citizens must always be ready to defend their country and the freedoms it has given them.

During a Martin Luther King Jr. Day parade, students carry signs thanking Dr. King for his work in helping achieve civil rights for all.

To Find Out More

Here are some additional resources to help you learn more about civil rights:

 **Books**

Ditchfield, Christin. **Freedom of Speech.** Children's Press, 2004.

Duncan, Alice Faye. **The National Civil Rights Museum Celebrates Everyday People.** Troll Associates, 1999.

Pascoe, Elaine. **The Right to Vote.** Millbrook Press, 1997.

Quiri, Patricia Ryon. **The Bill of Rights.** Children's Press, 1998.

Sobel, Syl. **The U.S. Constitution and You.** Barron's Educational Series, Inc., 2001.

Organizations and Online Sites

Constitutional Rights Foundation
601 South Kingsley Drive
Los Angeles, CA 90005
http://www.crf-usa.org

This site helps young people understand the value of the Constitution and the Bill of Rights.

U.S. National Archives and Records Administration
700 Pennsylvania Ave. NW
Washington, DC 20408
http://www.archives.gov

On this site you can view the Declaration of Independence, the U.S. Constitution, and the Bill of Rights.

The White House
1600 Pennsylvania Avenue NW
Washington, D.C. 20500
http://www.whitehouse.gov

Check out *www.whitehouse kids.gov* for a virtual tour of the White House as well as games, quizzes, time-lines, and historical trivia.

Important Words

accessible able to be used by

accused someone charged with having done something wrong

boycotts acts of refusing to take part in something

citizens members of a particular country

confess to admit to doing wrong

debates discussions between people with different views

document paper containing important information

petitions letters signed by many people demanding change

principles basic rules that govern people's behavior

protesting speaking out against something

Index

Meet the Author

Christin Ditchfield is an author and conference speaker, and is host of the nationally syndicated radio program *Take It to Heart!* Her articles have been featured in magazines all over the world. A former elementary-school teacher, Christin has written more than twenty-five books for children on a wide range of topics, including sports, science, and history. She makes her home in Sarasota, Florida.

A fear of witchcraft spread through Salem Village. Many Puritans thought prayer would help save the village.

Reverend Parris believed the only way to help the girls was to remove the witch from the village. Most people believed only the victims knew who was casting a spell on them. The girls would not tell anyone the name of the witch.

Cures for Witchcraft

People responded to witchcraft in several ways. Many people believed prayer would help cure

A group of young girls in Salem Village became known as "afflicted girls." These girls acted strangely. They claimed witches had put a spell on them.

Stories about Tituba

Many stories claim Tituba played a large role in the Salem witch trials. Many people believed Tituba told the girls about a type of religion called voodoo. People thought these stories put ideas into the girls' heads. But historians do not believe this theory. No evidence exists that Tituba practiced voodoo activities.

Court record of
Tituba's statement

witchcraft. Reverend Parris spent his time praying. Meanwhile, Mary Sibley, a church member, asked Tituba to use magic to identify the witch. Both Mary and Tituba believed a special cake fed to the Parris' dog would identify the witch.

Before long, Ann Putnam and Elizabeth Hubbard began acting strangely. Six other girls also claimed to be victims of witchcraft. These girls, along with Betty and Abigail, became known throughout the area as the "afflicted girls."

Witches Named

Finally, Betty and Abigail named the first witch. They claimed Tituba practiced witchcraft. People easily believed she was a witch. She had proved she believed in witchcraft when she baked the cake for the Parris' dog. Tituba later confessed she had learned magic from a former employer who was a witch.

Claims of witchcraft terrified the people of Salem.

On February 25, 1692, Betty and Abigail accused Sarah Good and Sarah Osborne of witchcraft. The two women were unfriendly to others. It was not hard for the townspeople to imagine they were witches.

Charged with Witchcraft

Thomas Putnam was the father of young Ann. He brought charges against the accused witches, Sarah Good and Sarah Osborne. He went to the village leaders with Edward Putnam, Thomas Preston, and Joseph Hutchinson. Village leaders had to give their permission to arrest the accused women. Thomas Putnam filled out papers accusing the women of witchcraft.

Putnam's group arrested Sarah Good, Sarah Osborne, and Tituba on March 1, 1692. They took the women to the village meetinghouse. The judges held a hearing to hear the evidence. The charge was very serious. Witchcraft was punishable by death. The judges had to decide if the women should stand trial.

A large crowd gathered at the meetinghouse. Sarah Good and Sarah Osborne claimed innocence. Then, the afflicted girls began their strange behaviors. They claimed the women's specters were pinching and biting them. People believed a specter was a witch's spirit. Only the witch's victim could see the specter.

Tituba also claimed to be innocent. But she then changed her story. She admitted she was a witch. She said the other accused women were also witches. Tituba said that they had all flown on broomsticks. She added that she had seen other witches. She did not know their names. The judges believed all three women were witches. Sarah Good and Sarah Osborne were sent to jail to await trials.

Since Tituba confessed, the villagers believed she had broken Satan's hold. They thought she was no longer dangerous to the community. Tituba did not have to go to trial.

Witch Hunts in Europe

Witch-hunting peaked in Europe between 1580 and 1660. At least 100,000 people were executed in Europe on charges of witchcraft. The last witchcraft **execution** in Europe took place in Switzerland on June 17, 1782.

Trial by water was one method used to prove a witch's innocence or guilt. People believed a witch would float on the water. These "witches" were then hanged. Those people who sank in the water were declared innocent.

The trial by water method was used once in Hartford, Connecticut, during the 1660s. This form of testing ended before the Salem witch trials.

Chapter Three

Fear Spreads

By March 7, 1692, the accused witches were in jail. They awaited their trial. Yet, the girls continued to act strangely.

The villagers worried. The girls still seemed to be under a witch's spell. Tituba had said there were more witches in the village. Suddenly, neighbors began looking at each other with fear and distrust.

New Accusations

Thomas Putnam still led the witch hunt. His daughter claimed the specter of Martha Corey was hurting her. Martha was a respected member of the village. After several **accusations**, Martha was arrested.

Martha made it clear that she thought the girls were lying. She did not believe their claims.

People of all ages were accused of witchcraft and arrested during the Salem witch trials.

The Meetinghouse

The Puritans attended church services every Sunday. The services were held at the village meetinghouse. The meetinghouse was a plain, wooden building. In the winter, the villagers had no way to heat the building. They covered the windows with shutters, but the building was still cold. The shuttered windows also kept sunlight from lighting the meetinghouse. The minister read his sermons by candlelight. In 1692, the meetinghouse became the site of the witch-hunt trials.

During the hearing, the girls began howling.
The girls claimed Martha's specter was biting them.
They showed the judges bite marks on their arms.
Martha was taken to prison to await trial.

Next, the girls accused Rebecca Nurse.
Like Martha, Rebecca said the girls were telling lies.

Martha Corey was sent to prison. She was one of the first to be accused of witchcraft.

The judges respected Rebecca. They decided to free her. Then the girls began screaming that Rebecca's specter was hurting them. The judges changed their minds and sent Rebecca to prison.

Many people believed Satan left his mark on witches. The people accused of witchcraft were questioned and searched. This 1853 painting by T. H. Matteson is titled *Examination of a Witch*.

More Accusations

Next, the girls accused Sarah Good's 4-year-old daughter. Little Dorcas Good was too young to understand what was happening. She

admitted that both she and her mother were witches. Dorcas was taken away in chains.

By late March, John Proctor had heard enough. His servant, Mary Warren, was one of the girls claiming to be under a witch's spell. He was angry. He believed the girls were causing trouble.

The girls immediately claimed they could see the specter of Proctor's wife, Elizabeth. When Proctor tried to defend his wife, the girls accused him of witchcraft. Both John and Elizabeth Proctor were arrested.

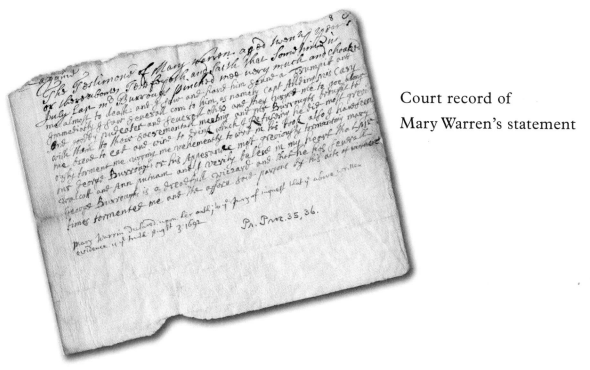

Court record of
Mary Warren's statement

Confession

The claims of witchcraft continued during the spring. The trials had not begun, but fear spread. People accused their enemies, neighbors, and family members of witchcraft.

By April, Mary Warren could no longer keep silent. She told the court that she and the other girls were faking their behavior. The other girls turned on Mary. They accused her of witchcraft. Mary was arrested and brought before the judges. Mary quickly changed her story. She said the girls were telling the truth. Mary was released from jail and never again spoke out against the other girls.

Statements made by the young girls brought fear to Salem Village. Soon, family and friends began to accuse one another of witchcraft.

Chapter Four

The Trials

On May 27, William Phipps, governor of the Massachusetts Bay Colony, formed an emergency court. The court was called the Court of Oyer and Terminer. Judges were told to reach quick, final decisions on each case. Phipps appointed a panel of seven judges. He then named William Stoughton as the chief judge.

The girls' behavior and their claims served as the main evidence. Cotton Mather, a leading Massachusetts minister, warned the panel. He wanted the judges to be careful about using specters as evidence. Mather was an expert on witchcraft. Mather believed Satan was tricking the girls into thinking they saw a witch's specter.

A panel of judges listened to people's statements. The judges then decided if the accused person was guilty or innocent of witchcraft.

The First Trial

The witch trials began June 2, 1692, with the trial of Bridget Bishop. Two men had accused her of sticking pins in rag dolls. This type of voodoo was practiced in the West Indies.

The trial did not go well for Bishop. When the girls gave their **testimony**, they thrashed about and shrieked. They claimed Bishop's specter was hurting them. The court found Bishop guilty. The judges sentenced her to hang at Gallows Hill near Salem.

Family members and friends feared the court's decision of guilt. People found guilty of witchcraft were sentenced to hang.

In Their Own Words

During the Salem witch trials, the court kept written records. Among these records are statements spoken by those men and women accused. "I am innocent of a witch," said Bridget Bishop during her trial.

Letters written during the witch trials are another source of information. In a letter to the judges, Mary Easty wrote before her death, " . . . if it be possible no more innocent blood be shed . . . I am clear of this **sin**."

Spectral Evidence

After Bishop's trial, the judges thought carefully about using spectral evidence. They wondered if Satan could take the form of an innocent person to trick the girls. Chief Justice William Stoughton insisted that spectral evidence be allowed. The girls could claim a witch's specter was biting or pinching them. The girls' claims would be enough evidence to charge a person with witchcraft.

Chapter Five

Guilty!

As the trials continued, it became clear that they were unfair. During Sarah Good's trial, a girl screamed that Good's specter was trying to stab her. Then the girl showed the court a broken knife blade. An observer stepped forward and said the blade was his. He had broken it earlier. The judges warned the girl not to lie again. But the judges continued to believe everything else she said. Good was charged as a witch. She was sentenced to die.

During Rebecca Nurse's trial, the court ruled that she was innocent. Suddenly, her accusers began howling that her specter was trying to kill them. A person in court claimed that one of the girls was sticking pins in her own knee. But the judges believed the girls.

The judges changed their decision to guilty.

People accused of witchcraft tried to defend themselves. The judges often did not believe them and announced decisions of guilt.

Spectral evidence continued to play the greatest role in the trials. The accuser's word was accepted without doubt. In most cases, there was no way to prove whether the girls were lying or telling the truth.

Bridget Bishop was taken to Gallows Hill and hanged.

Lord's Prayer

Puritans believed that a witch could not say the Lord's Prayer without stumbling over the words. Before his hanging, Reverend George Burroughs said the complete prayer, but he was hanged anyway.

The Executions

Bridget Bishop was the first person charged with witchcraft and sentenced to hang. On June 10, officials took Bishop from prison and loaded her into a cart. She was taken to Gallows Hill and hanged from a tree.

The second set of hangings took place on July 19. Five women, including Sarah Good and Rebecca Nurse, were hanged. Their dead bodies were cut down and tossed into a gap in the rocks on Gallows Hill.

On August 19, five more people were hanged. George Burroughs, once a minister in Salem Village, was put to death. John Proctor was also hanged. His wife, Elizabeth, was to be spared until after her baby was born.

The final hangings took place on September 22. Martha Corey and seven other people were hanged at Gallows Hill.

Unusual Death

Giles Corey also met his death in September. During his hearing, he pleaded not guilty. But Corey refused to be part of the trial. According to law, a person who refused to stand for trial was

Giles Corey memorial stone

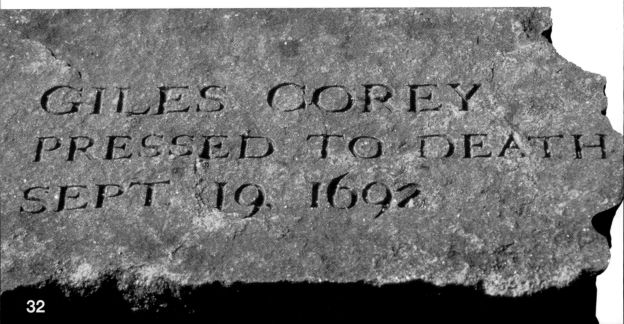

sentenced to death. Corey was placed on his back in a nearby field with a board on his chest. Heavy rocks were piled on top, slowly crushing him to death. This was the only time this form of punishment was used in the colony.

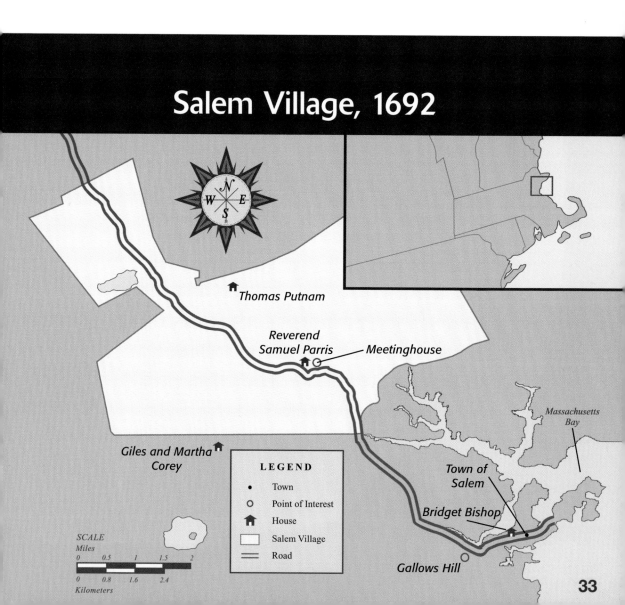

Salem Village, 1692

Thomas Putnam

Reverend
Samuel Parris — Meetinghouse

Massachusetts
Bay

Giles and Martha
Corey

LEGEND
- • Town
- ○ Point of Interest
- ♠ House
- ▢ Salem Village
- ═ Road

Town of
Salem

Bridget Bishop

SCALE
Miles
0   0.5   1   1.5   2

0   0.8   1.6   2.4
Kilometers

Gallows Hill

Chapter Six

Sanity Returns

By the fall of 1692, nearly every family in the Salem area had been touched in some way by the witch hunt. Twenty people had been killed because of witchcraft charges. As many as 350 more people were accused of witchcraft.

Public opinion was starting to change. People were beginning to doubt the girls. Some believed Satan was tricking the girls. Others thought the girls were lying on purpose.

The girls began accusing some of Massachusetts' richest and most powerful people. After the girls accused the wife of Governor Phipps, he began to stop the witch hunts. On October 11, Governor Phipps ended the arrests for witchcraft. By the end of October, he closed the court that heard the cases.

By fall, many began to doubt the girls' statements. This drawing by Howard Pyle shows a court scene during the Salem witch trials.

A new court heard the remaining cases. Spectral evidence was not allowed. In January 1693, the remaining cases were heard. At least 50 people were accused. Only three people were found guilty and sentenced to death. Governor Phipps later took back their death sentences and set them free.

Governor William Phipps ordered that the Salem witch trials be stopped. In May 1693, he dropped the charges of those people still in prison on the charge of witchcraft.

Destroyed Lives

Nineteen people had been hanged for witchcraft during the Salem witch trials. One man had been killed for not agreeing to take part in the court process. Other people, including Sarah Osborne, died while in prison.

Most of the accused survived the witch hunt, but they had suffered. Before they could be released from prison, they had to pay a jailer's fee. This fee paid for fuel, clothing, food, legal paperwork, and court costs.

Many families lost everything they owned during the witch hunt. When a person was found guilty, the person charged lost the right to own possessions. The sheriff took all farm animals and household goods. Even if the accused were cleared of charges, it was not easy for them to rebuild their lives. Many villagers continued to believe the accused really were witches.

Changing the Records

The freed prisoners asked two things of the government. They wanted their records wiped clean of witchcraft charges. They also wanted their belongings returned.

In 1710, the government of the Massachusetts Bay Colony reversed the charges of the people who died as a result of the witch hunt. The government also made payments to 24 families. These families had lost family members or property during the witch hunt.

Some people tried to make up for their part in the witch trials. Judge Samuel Sewall apologized for his role. Tituba took back her whole story. She confessed that Reverend Parris forced her to lie. In 1706, Ann Putnam confessed in church. She said none of the stories had been true. She claimed Satan had tricked her.

Beyond the Salem Witch Trials

The girls who were responsible for the tragedy in Salem Village were never punished. Their actions harmed many, but they were not held responsible.

Samuel Sewall
apologized for his role in
the Salem witch trials.
He had served as a judge
on the Court of Oyer
and Terminer.

The Salem witch trials changed the lives of the villagers. Even the American court system changed. The Salem witch trials were the last time spectral evidence was ever allowed in trials.

In 1992, a memorial was completed in memory of those who died during the Salem witch trials. The memorial stands in Danvers, Massachusetts.

Witch Hunts in U.S. History

In 1953, Arthur Miller's play *The Crucible* appeared on Broadway. The play was based on the 1692 Salem witch trials.

Miller added his own ideas in the play. The subject of the play was the McCarthy hearings that took place in the 1950s.

During the 1950s, Senator Joseph McCarthy led a committee that accused people of belonging to the Communist Party. **Communism** was the government system of the former Soviet Union. At the time, the United States and the Soviet Union did not have good relations. McCarthy thought people who believed in communism were enemies of the United States. The committee often had little evidence against the people it accused. The McCarthy hearings ruined many people's careers.

Today, Salem Village is known as Danvers, Massachusetts. Many years have passed, but the Salem witch trials are remembered. A memorial stands in Danvers. This memorial was built in memory of those who died during the witch trials.

TIME LINE

Sarah Good and Sarah Osborne plead innocent of witchcraft, but Tituba pleads guilty; the women are sent to jail to await trial.

Betty Parris and Abigail Williams begin acting strangely.

Bridget Bishop is hanged on Gallows Hill; her death is the first of the Salem witch trials.

January 1692 February 1692 March 1692 May 1692 June 1692

Sarah Good, Sarah Osborne, and Tituba are named as witches.

William Phipps, governor of the Massachusetts Bay Colony, appoints an emergency court of judges; this court is called the Court of Oyer and Terminer.

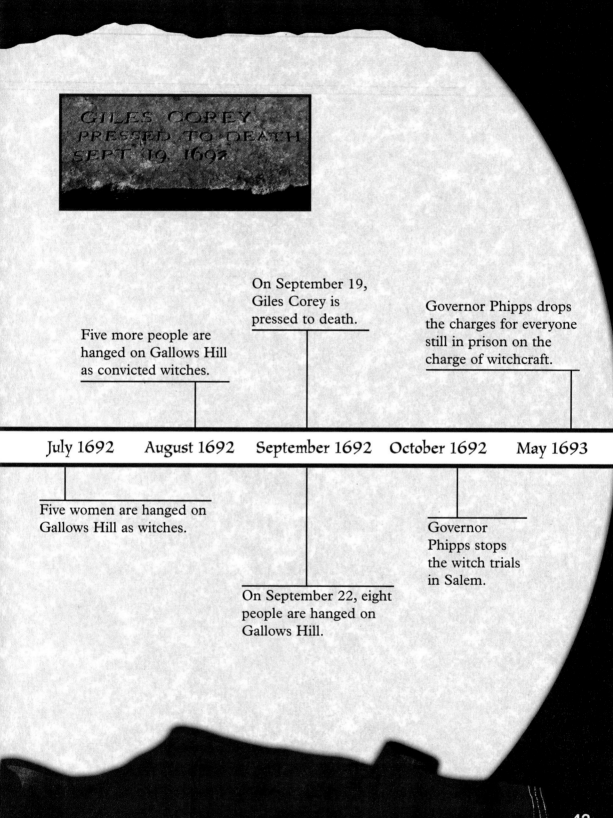

GILES COREY
PRESSED TO DEATH
SEPT 19, 1692

On September 19, Giles Corey is pressed to death.

Governor Phipps drops the charges for everyone still in prison on the charge of witchcraft.

Five more people are hanged on Gallows Hill as convicted witches.

| July 1692 | August 1692 | September 1692 | October 1692 | May 1693 |

Five women are hanged on Gallows Hill as witches.

Governor Phipps stops the witch trials in Salem.

On September 22, eight people are hanged on Gallows Hill.

Glossary

accusation (ak-yoo-ZAY-shuhn)—a charge of wrongdoing

colony (KOL-uh-nee)—a territory that has been settled by people from another country

communism (KOM-yuh-niz-uhm)—a way of organizing a country so that all the land, houses, and factories belong to the government and the profits are shared by all

execution (ek-suh-KYOO-shuhn)—being put to death as punishment for a crime

Puritan (PYOOR-uh-tuhn)—a member of a group of Protestants in the 16th and 17th centuries who followed a strict moral code

Satan (SAY-tuhn)—the devil or an evil spirit

sin (SIN)—bad or evil behavior that goes against moral or religious laws

testimony (TESS-tuh-moh-nee)—a statement given by a witness in a court of law

Read More

Asirvatham, Sandy. *The Salem Witch Trials.* Great Disasters, Reforms and Ramifications. Philadelphia: Chelsea House, 2002.

Dolan, Edward F. *The Salem Witch Trials.* Kaleidoscope. New York: Benchmark Books/Marshall Cavendish, 2002.

Kallen, Stuart A. *The Salem Witch Trials.* The World History Series. San Diego: Lucent Books, 1999.

MacBain, Jenny. *The Salem Witch Trials: A Primary Source History of the Witchcraft Trials in Salem, Massachusetts.* Primary Sources in American History. New York: Rosen, 2003.

Wilson, Lori Lee. *The Salem Witch Trials.* How History Is Invented. Minneapolis: Lerner, 1997.

Useful Addresses

John Ward House
East India Square
Salem, MA 01970
Visitors to this museum tour will learn about life during the Salem witch trials. The John Ward house was built in Salem in 1684.

Salem Village
Witchcraft Memorial
176 Hobart Street
Danvers, MA 01923
This memorial honors all of the 1692 witchcraft trial victims; it is located across the street from where the original Salem Village meetinghouse stood.

Salem Witch Museum
Washington Square
Salem, MA 01970
This Salem museum uses stage sets with life-size figures to give a brief history of the Salem witch trials of 1692.

Salem Witch Trials Memorial
Liberty Street
Salem, MA 01970
This memorial was dedicated in 1992 to the victims of the Salem witch trials of 1692.

Internet Sites

FactHound offers a safe, fun way to find Internet sites related to this book. All of the sites on FactHound have been researched by our staff.

Here's how:
1. Visit *www.facthound.com*
2. Type in this special code **0736824642** for age-appropriate sites.
   Or enter a search word related to this book for a more general search.
3. Click on the Fetch It button.

FactHound will fetch the best sites for you!

Index